THE NIGHTLIFE MASTREO
MASTREO

A BIOGRAPHY OF SACHA LORD

AMELIA ELOISE

INTRODUCTION

With neon lights illuminating the streets and heart palpitating beats, Sacha Lord becomes a visionary force in Manchester's nightlife. Sacha was born and raised in Manchester, where he finds inspiration and a playground among the city's energetic neighbourhoods.

Sacha has always had a strong love for music and nightlife. He spends his evenings absorbing in the unique sounds of the city's diversified music scene, immersing himself in the beats that echo through the streets. Here, amid the dance floors and dimly lit clubs, Sacha finds his calling: to create moments that are alive with vitality and energy, to create experiences that go beyond the ordinary.

Driven by ambition and unwavering determination, Sacha embarks on a mission to establish his own niche in the world of nightlife. Possessing an unending creative spirit and astute business sense, he sets out on a quest that will fundamentally alter Manchester's cultural milieu.

4

Sacha Lord is a household name in the nightlife scene thanks to his founding of renowned events like The Warehouse Project and Parklife festival. His gatherings attract large numbers of people, converting abandoned warehouses into vibrant centres of culture and music.

However, Sacha's influence goes beyond the dance floor. In his capacity as Greater Manchester's Night Time Economy Adviser, he takes a leading position in promoting the nightlife of the city and stressing its significance as a major cultural and economic force.

Sacha Lord's narrative evolves with each beat, demonstrating the transformational power of music and the unwavering spirit of a visionary master.

CHAPTER 1

The Rise of Sacha Lord

In the heart of Manchester, Sacha Lord is born into a family that believes in the transformative power of music and community. As Sacha grows up in the busy city neighbourhoods, he is surrounded by a diverse range of sounds and rhythms that influence his early recollections. Sacha's diverse musical background, which includes everything from the throbbing beats of electronic music to the lyrical melodies of Motown, sets the groundwork for his future pursuits.

Sacha has an unwavering love for music even as a small child. His ears trained to pick up even the smallest details in sound, he spends his days scouring through vinyl recordings in neighbourhood record stores. In this setting, with the mesmerising hum of turntables and the crackling static of vinyl, Sacha finds his true calling: curating extraordinary experiences.

Motivated by an unwavering drive to spread his passion for music among others, Sacha embarks on a self-exploration trip. He immerses himself in the vibrant music scene of Manchester, going to warehouse parties and underground performances that are teeming with inventiveness and raw energy. With other music lovers all around her, Sacha experiences a unique sense of community in these darkly illuminated settings.

Sacha's drive to make a lasting impact on the world is growing along with his enthusiasm for music. Driven by a fervent desire and a steadfast faith in his own abilities, Sacha aims to create an event that will bring together music enthusiasts from diverse backgrounds and expand the parameters of the nightlife landscape.

With an unending creative imagination and a strong sense of entrepreneurial spirit, Sacha starts to build the foundation for what will soon be his greatest accomplishment. He sees an event that will push the boundaries of innovation and originality while celebrating the rich musical tradition of Manchester, drawing inspiration from the city's strong vitality in the music scene.

Thus, Sacha Lord's idea is realised in the summer of 2010 with the opening of the Parklife festival. Parklife, a festival that attracts music enthusiasts from all over the UK, swiftly makes a name for itself against the breathtaking background of Manchester's Heaton Park.

However, Sacha's adventure is far from ended. Encouraged by Parklife's success, he embarks on a new endeavour: organising an event that would push the limits of the nightlife landscape and rethink what immersive entertainment means.

Thus, The Warehouse Project begins in the winter of 2006. The Warehouse Project, which is housed in a massive industrial warehouse outside of Manchester, swiftly establishes itself as a destination for music lovers, attracting some of the biggest names in electronic music to its revered halls.

However, Sacha's influence goes beyond the warehouse walls. He becomes a major player in Manchester's nightlife scene as the creator of The Warehouse Project and Parklife festival, reshaping the city's cultural landscape and solidifying its standing as a centre of musical invention and originality.

CHAPTER 2

Redefining Manchester's Nightlife

Sacha Lord is a prominent figure in Manchester's nightlife scene, a visionary who has had a unique influence on the city's cultural landscape. His story is one of passion, tenacity, and an unwavering quest of perfection as he turned unremarkable locations into vibrant centres of creativity and vitality. The Warehouse Project and the Parklife festival are two significant occasions that will always be remembered.

When Sacha co-founded The Warehouse Project (WHP) in the early 2000s, he made his first steps into the events and nightlife industries. The idea was straightforward yet revolutionary: turn abandoned buildings into transient locations for electronic music events, giving music lovers and club goers an immersive experience. But there were several obstacles in the way of WHP's establishment.

Finding appropriate locations for the events was one of the first challenges Sacha had to overcome. An abundance of deserted factories and warehouses from Manchester's industrial heritage were waiting to be transformed. It was difficult, nevertheless, to persuade property owners to rent these areas for a short time. Many were reluctant to take the chance because they doubted that such gatherings would be successful.

Sacha persisted in presenting his idea to landowners, highlighting the potential cultural and financial advantages for the city. His persistence paid off in 2006 when he was able to obtain WHP's first location, which signalled the start of a revolution in Manchester's nightlife.

The Warehouse Project's triumph opened the door for Sacha's next big project, the Parklife festival. When Parklife was first introduced in 2010, its goal was to replicate the excitement of WHP in an outdoor festival environment by presenting a varied roster of performers on several stages. But planning a big festival came with a whole other set of difficulties.

It was crucial to secure the ideal location, and Sacha discovered Heaton Park, a vast green area outside of Manchester, to be the ideal choice. It was no easy task, though, to manage the logistical challenges of organising an event of this size. Sacha and his team had to deal with a wide range of difficulties, from booking big-name acts and handling ticket sales to working with local authorities to guarantee safety and security.

However, Sacha's exceptional talent selection skills and his acute awareness of his audience's needs distinguished Parklife from other festivals. Parklife encapsulated Manchester's vibrant music scene by bringing together underground talent from different genres with major artists, drawing thousands of fans from all across the UK and beyond.

Even with its quick ascent, Parklife faced some challenges along the road. The festival faced threats from unfavourable weather, logistical difficulties, and even last-minute cancellations. But thanks to his tenacity and resolve, Sacha was able to weather every storm and come out stronger and more determined than before.

The Warehouse Project and Parklife have grown to be synonymous with Manchester's cultural revival over time, drawing praise from all over the world and solidifying Sacha's standing as a trailblazer in the events sector. These events, which have included ground-breaking performances by well-known performers as well as given up-and-coming talent a stage, have made a lasting impression on the cultural landscape of the city.

Sacha's story demonstrates the strength of vision and tenacity in the face of difficulty. He has changed the story of Manchester's nightlife industry and turned abandoned buildings into thriving cultural hotspots because to his persistent drive to pushing boundaries and producing remarkable experiences.

Sacha Lord continues to push the boundaries and redefine the possibilities of event production, making him a source of inspiration for aspiring business owners and cultural innovators alike. He demonstrates that anything is possible in the dynamic world of nightlife and entertainment if one has passion, tenacity, and a relentless pursuit of excellence.

CHAPTER 3

Manchester's Maestro of Music and Culture

Sacha Lord is a prominent player in Manchester's cultural scene, a maestro who skillfully orchestrates symphonies of music, art, and communal spirit. His rise from modest beginnings to a prominent role in the city's nightlife and cultural scene is evidence of his enthusiasm, foresight, and steadfast dedication to highlighting the transformative potential of music.

Growing up in the city's many and colourful neighbourhoods during his early years, Sacha played a significant role in Manchester's music and cultural scene. He was enthralled with the city's streets' kaleidoscope of sounds and rhythms from an early age, from the throbbing rhythms of the emerging electronic music scene to the anthemic beats of Oasis.

Sacha's love of music and his ambition to create immersive experiences that honoured the city's rich cultural legacy were sparked by this rich musical tapestry. Sacha started his career in the nightlife sector in the late 1990s, throwing a number of club nights and events that broke rules and challenged norms.

Sacha's ability to bring together artists, venues, and local communities to create remarkable experiences that connect with audiences throughout the globe is one of his most distinctive qualities. Over the course of his career, Sacha has collaborated with a wide range of musicians, from up-and-coming stars to well-known figures, demonstrating the depth and breadth of Manchester's music scene.

A well-known Manchester band called The Stone Roses was one of Sacha's most prominent partnerships. Sacha was instrumental in planning the band's much awaited reunion shows at Manchester's Heaton Park in 2012. Attracting tens of thousands of fans from across the world, the performances were a historic milestone in Manchester's music history and marked a victorious return for The Stone Roses.

In addition to working with musicians, Sacha has played a significant role in converting Manchester's venues into thriving cultural centres that honour the city's music industry. Sacha has dedicated countless hours to organising concerts that highlight the variety and inventiveness of Manchester's music culture, whether in storied locations like Manchester Arena or venerable clubs like The Hacienda.

The Warehouse Project was one of Sacha's most ambitious projects when it was founded in 2006. The idea was straightforward but revolutionary: turn vacant industrial areas into transient locations for immersive electronic music performances. With its innovative artist lineup and exhilarating environment, The Warehouse Project swiftly rose to prominence in Manchester's nightlife, drawing thousands of music lovers.

Sacha is dedicated to promoting Manchester's music scene and doesn't stop at conventional venues. In addition, he has supported neighborhood-based music events and local musicians, showcasing the wide range of musical ability in the area.

The Greater Manchester Music Fund is one such programme that Sacha assisted in starting to assist up-and-coming artists and musical endeavours in the area. To ensure that Manchester's thriving music industry survives for many years to come, the fund offers financial support to musicians and organisations that promote and celebrate the city's rich musical history.

Beyond his partnerships with musicians and venues, Sacha has had a significant influence on Manchester's music and arts scenes. Additionally, he has been a strong supporter of the idea that the city's nightlife and culture play a crucial role in defining its character. In her capacity as the inaugural Night Time Economy Advisor for Manchester, Sacha was instrumental in elevating the city's nightlife and guaranteeing its continued vibrancy as an all-encompassing area.

Sacha Lord has shaped Manchester's music and culture scene with his unshakable passion and ceaseless efforts, creating an enduring impression on the city's landscape. From his early days of club night organisation to his innovative work with The Warehouse Project and Parklife festival, Sacha has inspired many artists, audiences, and communities with his love of music and dedication to honouring Manchester's cultural legacy.

Sacha Lord is a shining example of innovation, teamwork, and community spirit in the music and cultural industries. He is constantly pushing the envelope and making a lasting impact on Manchester's music scene.

CHAPTER 4

Advocacy for Greater Manchester's Vibrant Culture

Sacha Lord is a dedicated advocate for the nighttime economy and the dynamic cultural environment it symbolises, and she is a beacon of change in the heart of Greater Manchester's nightlife. Sacha has devoted his time as Greater Manchester's Night Time Economy Adviser to tackling regulatory matters, encouraging teamwork, and promoting the wide range of companies and communities that make up the vibrant nightlife sector in the area.

Long before Sacha was named Night Time Economy Adviser, he started his advocacy career. His broad background in event production and promotion, along with his enduring passion for music and nightlife, gave him a unique perspective on the difficulties facing Greater Manchester's nighttime economy.

The necessity for a more unified and inclusive approach to policing the nighttime economy was one of the major concerns that Sacha correctly highlighted early on. Sacha began attempting to close the divide between stakeholders and promote increased cooperation and understanding after seeing the significance of striking a balance between the interests of companies, citizens, and local government.

As the Night Time Economy Adviser, Sacha achieved a lot, but one of his greatest accomplishments was pushing Greater Manchester to establish the Night Time Economy (NTE) Task Force. The task force was formed in 2019 and brings together officials from the local government, businesses, law enforcement, and community organisations to discuss the particular issues that the nighttime economy faces and come up with creative solutions.

Sacha was instrumental in determining the NTE Task Force's goals and priorities by using his wealth of knowledge in the nightlife sector to guide the group's strategy. Sacha made sure that the task force's agenda took into account the interests and worries of all parties involved, from addressing matters of safety and security to fostering diversity and tolerance.

Under Sacha's direction, the NTE Task Force has made removing regulatory obstacles—which frequently impede the expansion and advancement of the nighttime economy—one of its primary areas of concern. Sacha has been an outspoken supporter of regulatory reform to better assist enterprises and promote a vibrant nighttime economy, citing outdated licencing laws and excessive red tape as examples of the problems.

Sacha's efforts in this area have paid off, as there have been real policy and regulatory reforms that streamline the licencing procedure, lower administrative barriers, and improve the climate for companies engaged in the night economy. Sacha has paved the road for more innovation and expansion in the thriving nightlife of Greater Manchester through his advocacy work.

Apart from his involvement in the NTE Task Force, Sacha has been a strong proponent of advancing diversity and inclusivity in the nocturnal economy. Acknowledging the significance of establishing secure and inclusive environments for every individual in the community, Sacha has supported programmes designed to promote increased diversity and inclusivity in the business.

The Greater Manchester Night-Time Economy Diversity & Inclusion Charter is one such programme that Sacha assisted in establishing in order to advance inclusivity and diversity in the nightlife industry in the area. A number of promises and principles are outlined in the charter with the goal of fostering a more diverse and inclusive evening economy. These include encouraging diversity in employment practices and making sure that venues and events are accessible to all community members.

Sacha's lobbying activity encompasses broader concerns of social responsibility and community engagement, going beyond the domain of policy and regulation. Sacha, who is aware of how the night economy shapes Greater Manchester's culture, has been a strong proponent of harnessing the energy of the night to drive constructive social change.

Supporting community-led activities and events that use music and nightlife's transformative capacity to address social issues and promote community togetherness has been one of Sacha's most significant contributions in this direction. Sacha has been in the forefront of efforts to leverage the nighttime economy as a platform for social good, spearheading everything from mental health awareness campaigns to fundraising events for neighbourhood charity.

In addition to influencing the regulations governing the nightlife in the area, Sacha's lobbying work as Night Time Economy Adviser for Greater Manchester has increased stakeholder unity and collaboration. Sacha has become a real champion of Greater Manchester's nighttime rebirth through his unceasing efforts to address regulatory difficulties, promote diversity and inclusivity, and harness the power of nightlife as a force for social change.

CHAPTER 5

A Journey of Entrepreneurial Innovation

Sacha Lord is a dynamic force in Manchester's nightlife, with a varied portfolio of projects spanning hospitality, entertainment, and beyond. She is a pioneer in event production and an astute businesswoman. In addition to changing the nightlife scene in Manchester, his inventive business methods and spirit of entrepreneurship have elevated him to the forefront of the city's cultural rebirth.

In the late 1990s, Sacha started his entrepreneurial adventure with the goal of going beyond event production to become more established in the nightlife business. His love of nightlife and music served as inspiration for a number of endeavours he undertook that would change the face of Manchester's entertainment industry.

2010 saw Sacha purchase Manchester's renowned Sankeys nightclub, which was one of his first business endeavours. When Sankeys first opened its doors in 1994, it was known for being a stronghold of the counterculture and underground music scene, drawing a wide range of musicians and music lovers. Sacha took advantage of the chance to revitalise the venerable nightclub, realising its potential as a cultural centre for the city's nightlife.

Sankeys saw a revolutionary rebirth under Sacha's direction, reclaiming its place as a trailblazing entity in Manchester's nightlife. Sacha's vision for Sankeys brought the venue to new heights of success, garnering it international praise and recognition as one of the world's top nightlife hotspots. This was achieved through the curation of avant-garde artist lineups and the introduction of creative event concepts.

Leveraging Sankeys' success, Sacha proceeded to broaden his commercial interests and increase his presence in the hospitality and entertainment domains. He is one of the cofounders of The Mancunian Way, a hospitality business that includes a wide range of establishments such as bars, restaurants, and hotels, all of which provide a distinctive fusion of immersive atmosphere, entertainment, and food.

The Refuge by Volta, a dynamic dining and entertainment destination nestled within the historic Principal Manchester hotel, is one of the main venues within The Mancunian Way network. A mainstay of Manchester's food and nightlife scene, The Refuge draws guests from near and far to revel in its unique offerings by fusing cutting-edge culinary concepts with live music, DJ performances, and immersive cultural experiences.

Apart from his endeavours in the hotel sector, Sacha has also proven to have an excellent sense of seeing and seizing new trends in the entertainment sector. He was a co-founder of Supernature, a boutique event that honours the fusion of culture, music, and art in distinctive outdoor venues, in 2017. Beyond the conventional bounds of music festivals, Supernature provides guests with a unique sensory experience that includes immersive art installations and diverse musical talent lineups.

Sacha's varied business endeavours are evidence of his inventive business strategy and spirit of entrepreneurship in the nightlife industry. Sacha has consistently shown a dedication to pushing limits and reinventing the possibilities of Manchester's cultural scene, whether it is through the revitalization of famous nightlife venues or the invention of novel concepts in hospitality and entertainment.

Sacha's entrepreneurial pursuits are driven by a profound love of music, culture, and community. His endeavours are more than just economic endeavours; they are manifestations of his vision for immersive experiences that celebrate the dynamic spirit of Manchester's nightlife, unite people, and encourage creativity.

Sacha's entrepreneurial path is proof of the strength of drive, creativity, and fortitude in the face of difficulty.

Sacha's journey from modest beginnings in the nightlife business to becoming a trailblazer in hospitality and entertainment serves as an uplifting illustration of what is possible when one has vision, perseverance, and an openness to change.

Sacha Lord continues to be a driving force in Manchester's cultural landscape, influencing the city's identity and making a lasting impression on its thriving nightlife scene as he pushes the boundaries of what is possible in the nightlife sector. His inventive business strategy and enterprising nature serve as a source of inspiration for budding businesspeople and cultural innovators alike, demonstrating that anything is achievable in the dynamic realm of entertainment and nightlife with enough drive, imagination, and willpower.

CHAPTER 6

A Cultural Legacy in Manchester

Sacha Lord is a prominent character in Manchester's cultural scene, distinguished not just by his groundbreaking work in the nightlife business but also by his wider cultural influence and charitable endeavours that have permanently altered the fabric of the city. Sacha's legacy is characterised by his steadfast dedication to community participation, social responsibility, and generosity, which have contributed to the development of Manchester's neighbourhoods and its cultural identity, above and beyond the throbbing beats and immersive experiences of the city's nightlife scene.

Sacha's path into philanthropy and community service stemmed from his enduring conviction that the arts and culture have the capacity to positively impact society. Sacha saw early on in his work that nightlife and cultural activities could be catalysts for social cooperation, community empowerment, and cultural enrichment. He began his career in event development and promotion.

Sacha's promotion of mental health awareness and welfare in the nightlife community is one of his most prominent charitable endeavours. Acknowledging the distinct demands and obstacles encountered by professionals in the nightlife sector, Sacha has been a strong proponent of raising mental health awareness and offering assistance and services to those requiring them.

Sacha has worked to create a culture of openness, empathy, and support within the nightlife community through programmes like the Greater Manchester Night-Time Economy Diversity & Inclusion Charter. This is done to make sure that people feel respected, valued, and supported in both their personal and professional lives.

Sacha has been actively involved in supporting a number of charitable organisations and community activities that aim to uplift and empower marginalised groups within Manchester, in addition to his advocacy work for mental health awareness. Sacha has proven to be deeply committed to giving back to the city that has influenced his profession and personality, as seen by his participation in fundraising events for local charities and partnerships with community organisations.

One of Sacha's most notable charitable pursuits is his sponsorship of programmes designed to combat poverty and homelessness in Manchester. Sacha has been a strong supporter of programmes that offer food, shelter, and other necessities to those who are homeless because she understands how crucial it is to address the underlying causes of homelessness and to help those who are in need.

Through collaborations with nonprofits and neighborhood-based projects, Sacha has contributed to the awareness-building and financial support-raising efforts for initiatives that offer critical assistance to those facing homelessness, such as outreach services, emergency shelters, and job training programmes. Through his efforts, the problem of homelessness in Manchester has gained attention, and measures to solve this urgent social issue have garnered support.

Apart from his charitable endeavours, Sacha's wider cultural influence encompasses his part in moulding Manchester's nightlife scene and cultural milieu. Being a co-founder of renowned festivals like Parklife and The Warehouse Project, Sacha has been instrumental in making Manchester a worldwide centre for the arts, music, and culture.

Sacha has brought attention to the richness and inventiveness of Manchester's cultural scene by using his creative approach to event production and promotion. As a result, the city's lively nightlife and cultural offerings have garnered recognition and praise from all over the world. Sacha's vision for Manchester's nightlife has contributed to the city's reputation as a vibrant and progressive cultural attraction. This includes everything from selecting artists for avant-garde lineups to developing immersive experiences that break rules and question expectations.

The continuing effects of Sacha's projects and the thriving cultural scene that flourishes in the city bear witness to his long legacy in moulding Manchester's nightlife landscape and cultural fabric. Sacha has made a significant impact on Manchester's cultural identity through his charitable work and creative approach to event production and promotion. His achievements have left an enduring impression on the city and will continue to shape Manchester's future as a major worldwide cultural centre.

Sacha Lord is still a driving force in Manchester's cultural scene, pushing the envelope in philanthropy, community involvement, and cultural innovation while encouraging others to see the positive social change that can be brought about through the arts and culture. His legacy is proof of the long-lasting influence of those who are dedicated to changing the world and leaving a lasting mark on the communities they work in.

CHAPTER 7

Vision for the Future

Sacha Lord is a leader and visionary in the rapidly changing nightlife and hospitality sectors. Her uncompromising dedication to excellence and innovative attitude will continue to define the industry's future. Sacha, a trailblazer in event production, hospitality, and cultural enhancement, envisions a futuristic nightlife and hospitality landscape that surpasses conventional venue limitations. This dynamic and holistic approach aims to reimagine the nightlife experience.

Sacha has a strong belief in the transformational power of culture, creativity, and community, which informs his vision for the future of nightlife and hospitality. Sacha has consistently aimed to create immersive experiences that captivate the senses, encourage connection, and celebrate the rich diversity of Manchester's cultural scene, from his early days in event production to his present endeavours in hospitality and entertainment.

One of Sacha's current initiatives, The Factory, is a groundbreaking cultural institution scheduled to debut in Manchester in 2022 and represents his vision for the future of hospitality and nightlife. The Factory, envisioned as a vibrant centre for the arts, music, and performance, is a daring step forward in Sacha's quest to design avant-garde venues that blur the boundaries between entertainment, culture, and the arts.

Sacha's goal of establishing a fully immersive, inclusive cultural experience that breaks down barriers and allows viewers to interact with art and culture in novel and surprising ways is at the core of The Factory. With topnotch shows and exhibitions, immersive art installations, and interactive activities, The Factory is poised to be a lively and dynamic venue that honours the creative spirit and promotes a feeling of belonging.

Beyond its actual location, Sacha's vision for The Factory encompasses a larger goal to assist and elevate up-and-coming artists, present a range of cultural viewpoints, and encourage cooperation and creativity among the arts community. By means of collaborations with nearby artists, artistic associations, and cultural establishments, Sacha hopes to establish a vibrant and all-encompassing arena that encourages artists to experiment, push limits, and meaningfully interact with viewers.

Apart from The Factory, Sacha's outlook on the future of hospitality and nightlife is evident in his continuous dedication to crafting inventive and immersive experiences that honour the liveliness and multiplicity of Manchester's cultural milieu. Sacha keeps pushing the envelope of what's feasible in the entertainment and nightlife industries, from his participation in legendary events like The Warehouse Project and Parklife festival to his broad portfolio of hospitality endeavours.

For the future of nightlife and hospitality, one of Sacha's objectives is to keep looking for fresh approaches to draw people in and produce unforgettable, deeply felt experiences. Through creative event ideas, thought-provoking cultural events, or state-of-the-art hospitality offers, Sacha hopes to uplift audiences, spark discussion, and promote a feeling of community and connection among the nightlife community.

Sacha's dedication to social responsibility and community involvement shapes his outlook on the future of nightlife and hospitality. Sacha is committed to creating environments and experiences that are inclusive, approachable, and socially conscious because she understands the importance that nightlife and hospitality have in defining the cultural identities of cities and communities.

Sacha is striving to promote diversity, equity, and inclusion within the nightlife and hospitality sectors through initiatives like the Greater Manchester Night-Time

Economy Diversity & Inclusion Charter. Her goal is to make sure that every member of the community feels appreciated, valued, and accepted. Sacha's goal is to create a dynamic and inclusive nightlife scene that reflects the vast diversity of Manchester's cultural terrain by promoting an environment of openness, collaboration, and mutual respect.

Sacha Lord is still a vibrant, forward-thinking influence in Manchester's cultural scene as he keeps pushing the envelope in terms of nightlife and hospitality. His continuous endeavours to improve the nighttime experience are evidence of his steadfast dedication to quality, creativity, and community involvement. Sacha is reshaping Manchester's nightlife and hotel industry with his creative leadership and innovative energy. He is bringing to life immersive experiences that highlight the strength of culture, creativity, and community.

CONCLUSION

A tribute to his imaginative leadership and unrelenting devotion to upgrading the nightlife experience is Sacha Lord's career in the nightlife sector. Sacha has made a lasting impact on Manchester's nightlife industry with his innovative work in event production, hospitality, and cultural enrichment, starting with his early days of club night organising.

Sacha transformed the way people experience music and culture as a co-founder of renowned events including The Warehouse Project and Parklife festival. She created immersive experiences that honour the richness and vitality of Manchester's cultural scene. His creative approach to event production and acute awareness of audience interaction have raised the bar for nightlife experiences all around the world.

In addition to his work in event production, Sacha has made a significant impact on Manchester's cultural landscape through his charitable work and community involvement. Sacha has shown a strong dedication to leveraging the nightlife and hospitality industries' potential to effect meaningful social change, as seen by her advocacy for diversity and inclusion programmes and promotion of mental health awareness within the nightlife community.

Sacha's lasting influence in the nightlife sector stems from his capacity to produce life-changing events that go beyond conventional limits and promote a feeling of community and connection. A new generation of businesspeople and cultural innovators have been motivated by Sacha's creative leadership to push the envelope in the nightlife and hospitality industries.

His influence will last for many years to come, influencing hospitality and nightlife in the future and permanently altering Manchester's and the world's cultural landscape. In addition to changing how people perceive music and culture, Sacha Lord's efforts as a nightlife maestro have improved the lives of innumerable people and communities and left a long-lasting legacy of social impact, innovation, and inventiveness in the nightlife sector.

Printed in Great Britain
by Amazon

38044626R00030